Flow & Flowers
Art Coloring Pages

By
Kathy Carman Henderson

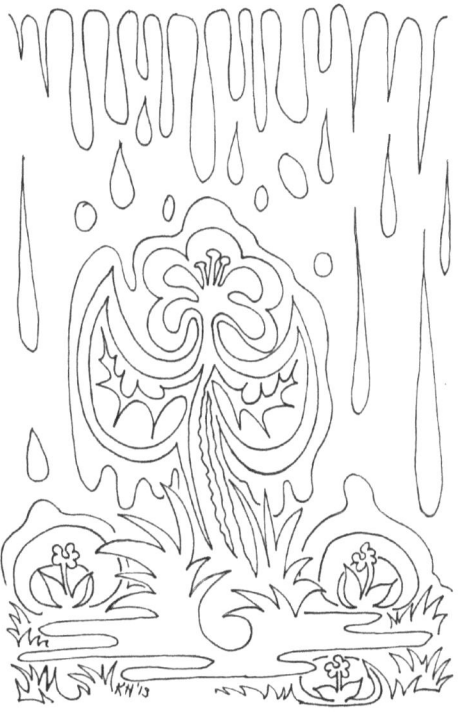

Kathy Carman Henderson

Copyright © 2013 Anna Kathleen (Carman) Henderson
All rights reserved.

ISBN-13: 978-1493717910
ISBN-10: 149371791X

Dear fellow artists,

    I have been drawing and coloring designs like these for years. With designs I especially like, I have often wanted to try completing the same design in different color schemes. That idea was the start of this coloring book. I also wanted to share my love for color and shape with others. So ... here are some freehand drawings to turn into your own creations. There are two copies of each design, so you can do what I've always wanted to do – use different color schemes on the same design.

    I use colored pencils, but feel free to try sharp crayons, watercolors, or any other medium. If you use something like pencils which require firm pressure, you may want to put a piece of cardboard under your drawing, so the surface of the next design isn't damaged. Or carefully tear out the page you are working on and attach to a clipboard. Creating these designs is a soothing process for me; I hope completing them will be a satisfying process for you.

    Have fun and God bless you,

    Kathy Carman Henderson

Kathy Carman Henderson

Flow & Flowers

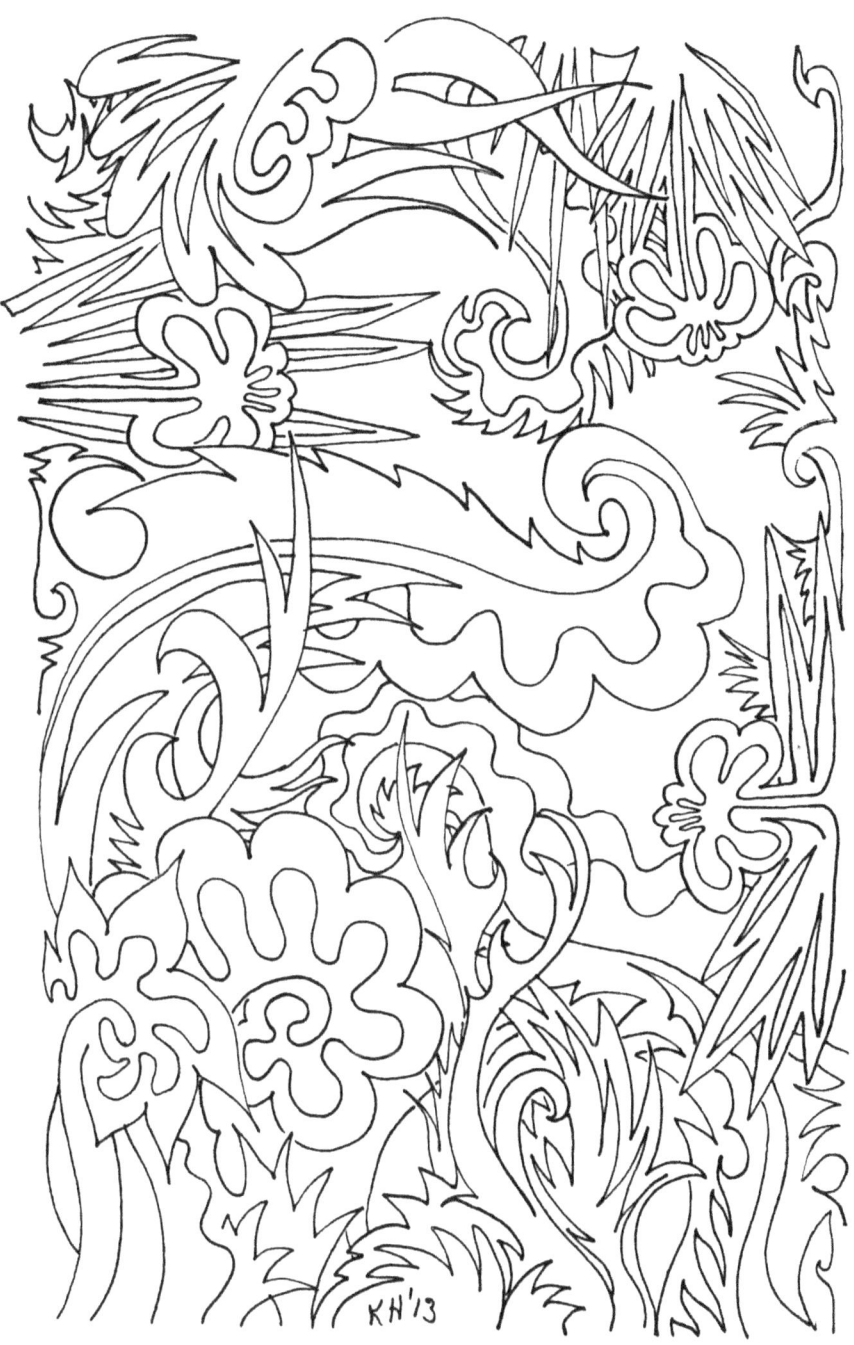

Kathy Carman Henderson

Flow & Flowers

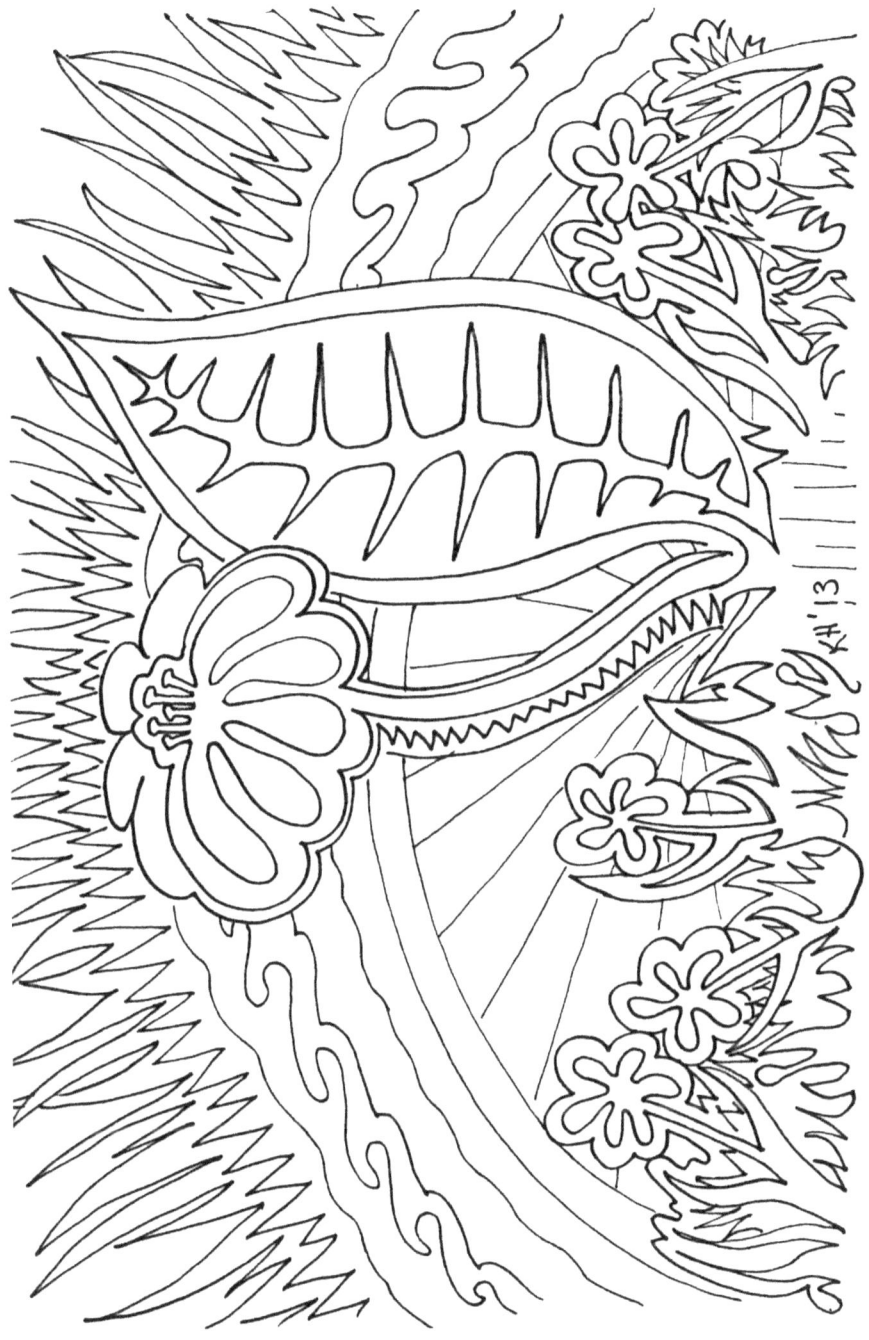

Kathy Carman Henderson

Flow & Flowers

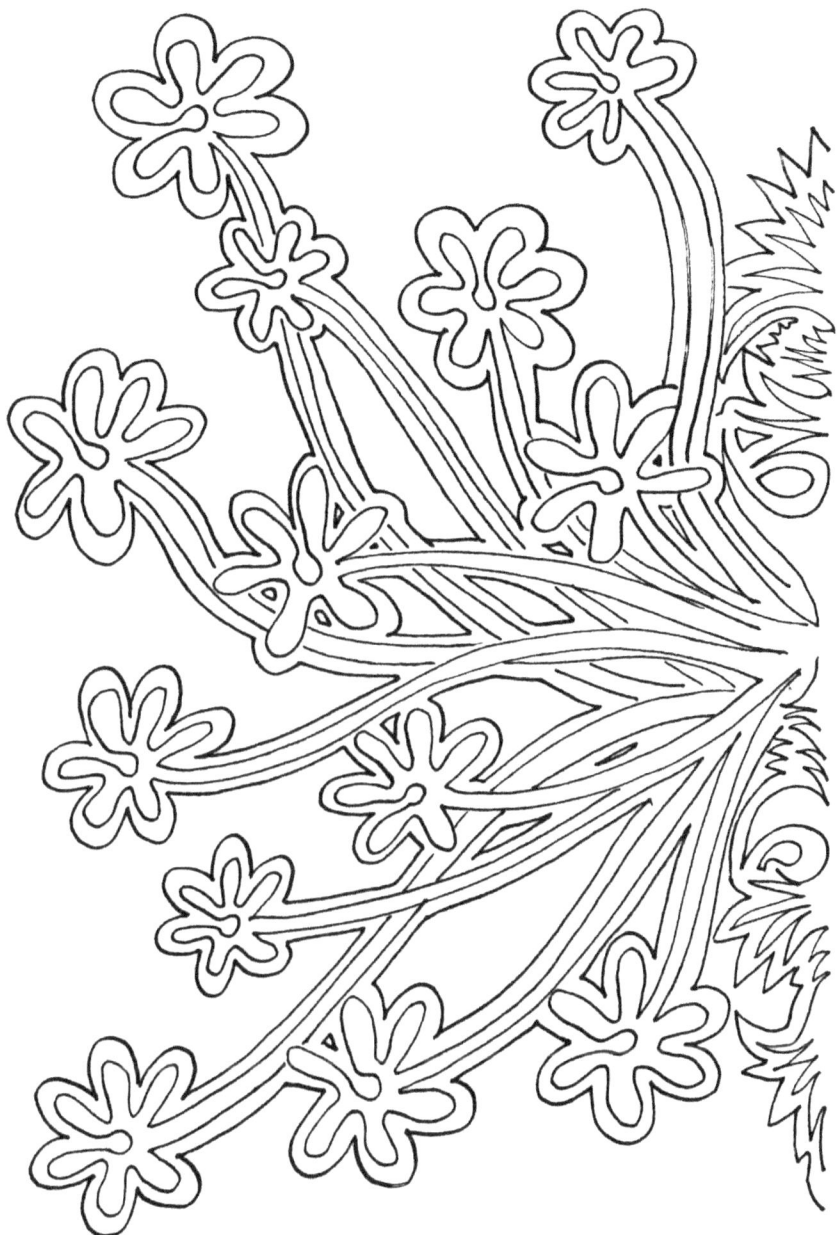

Kathy Carman Henderson

Flow & Flowers

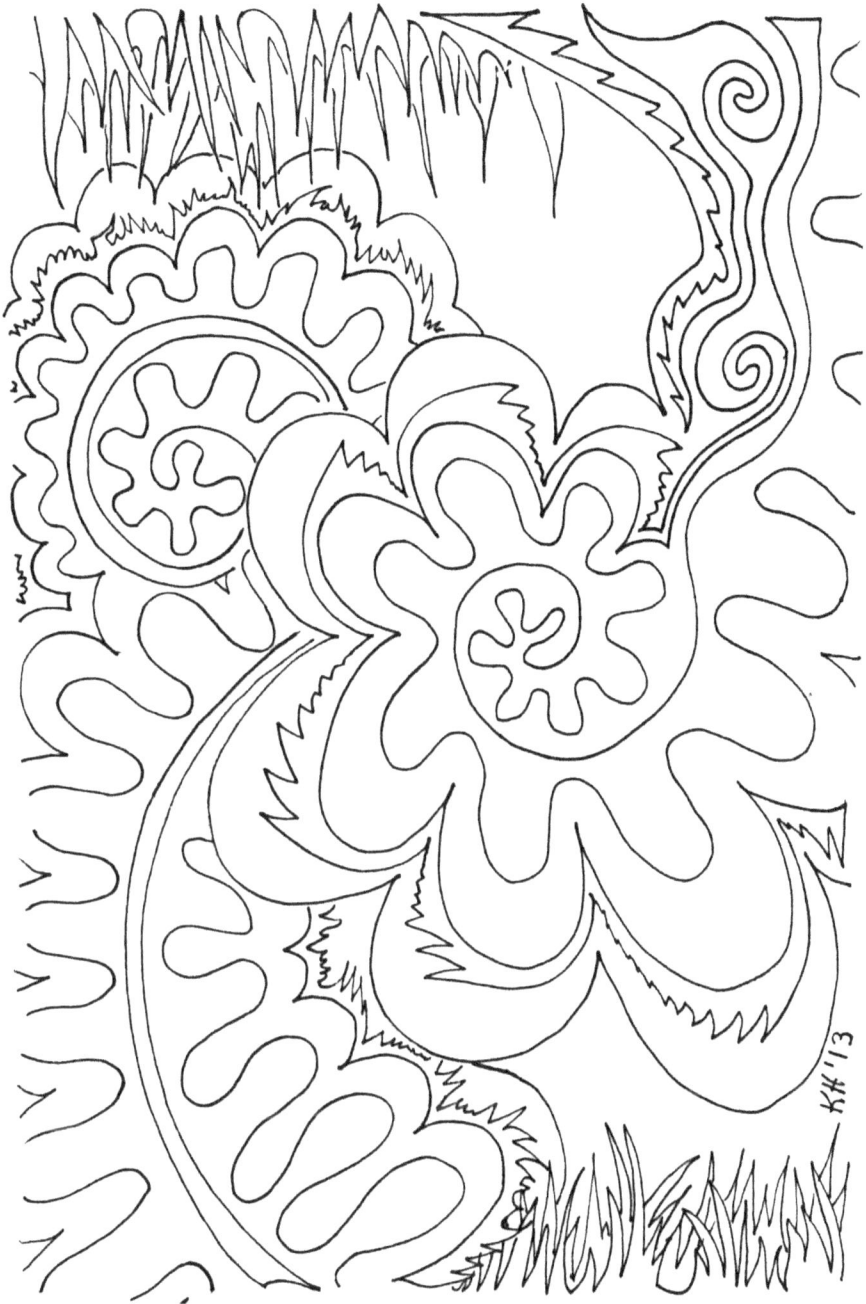

Kathy Carman Henderson

Flow & Flowers

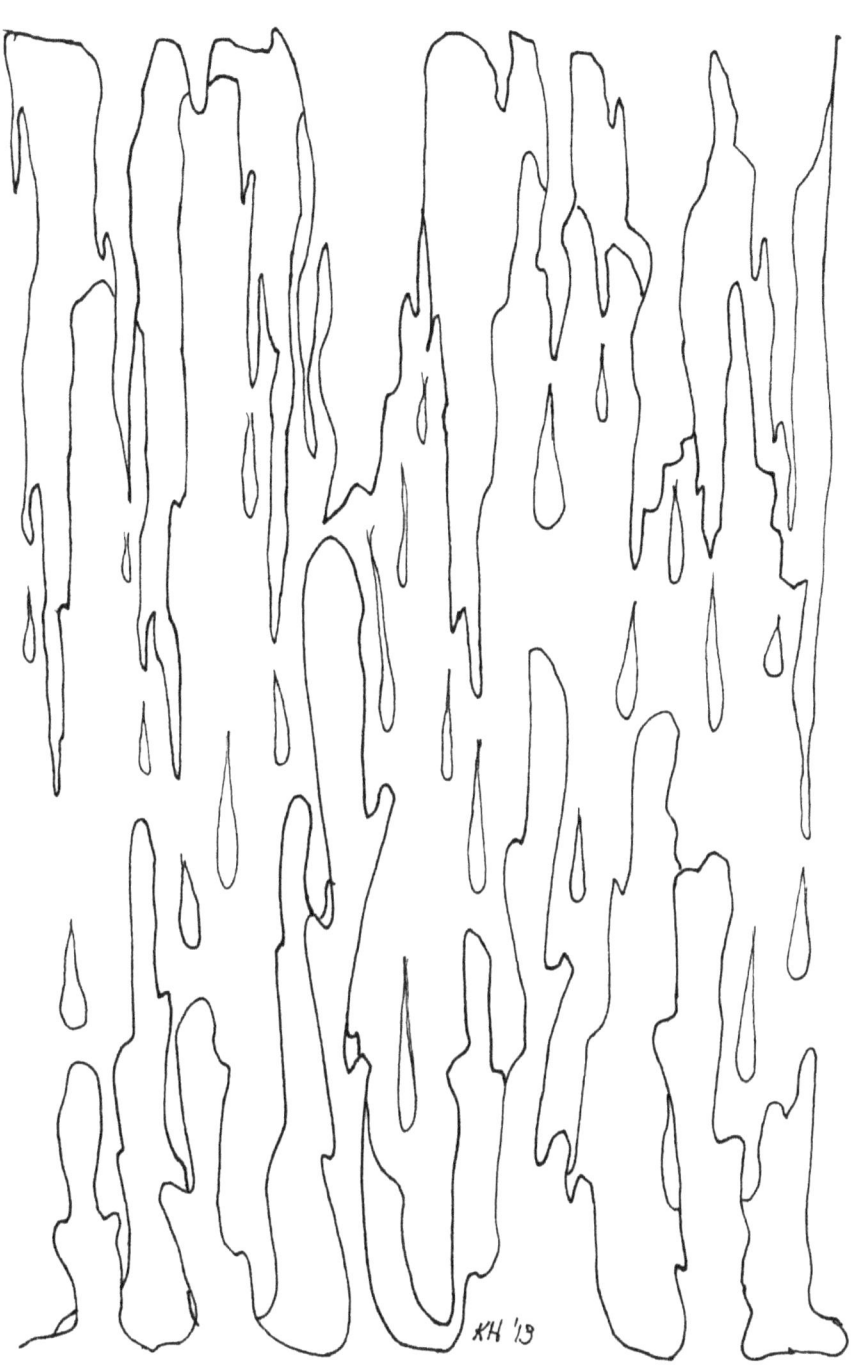

Kathy Carman Henderson

Flow & Flowers

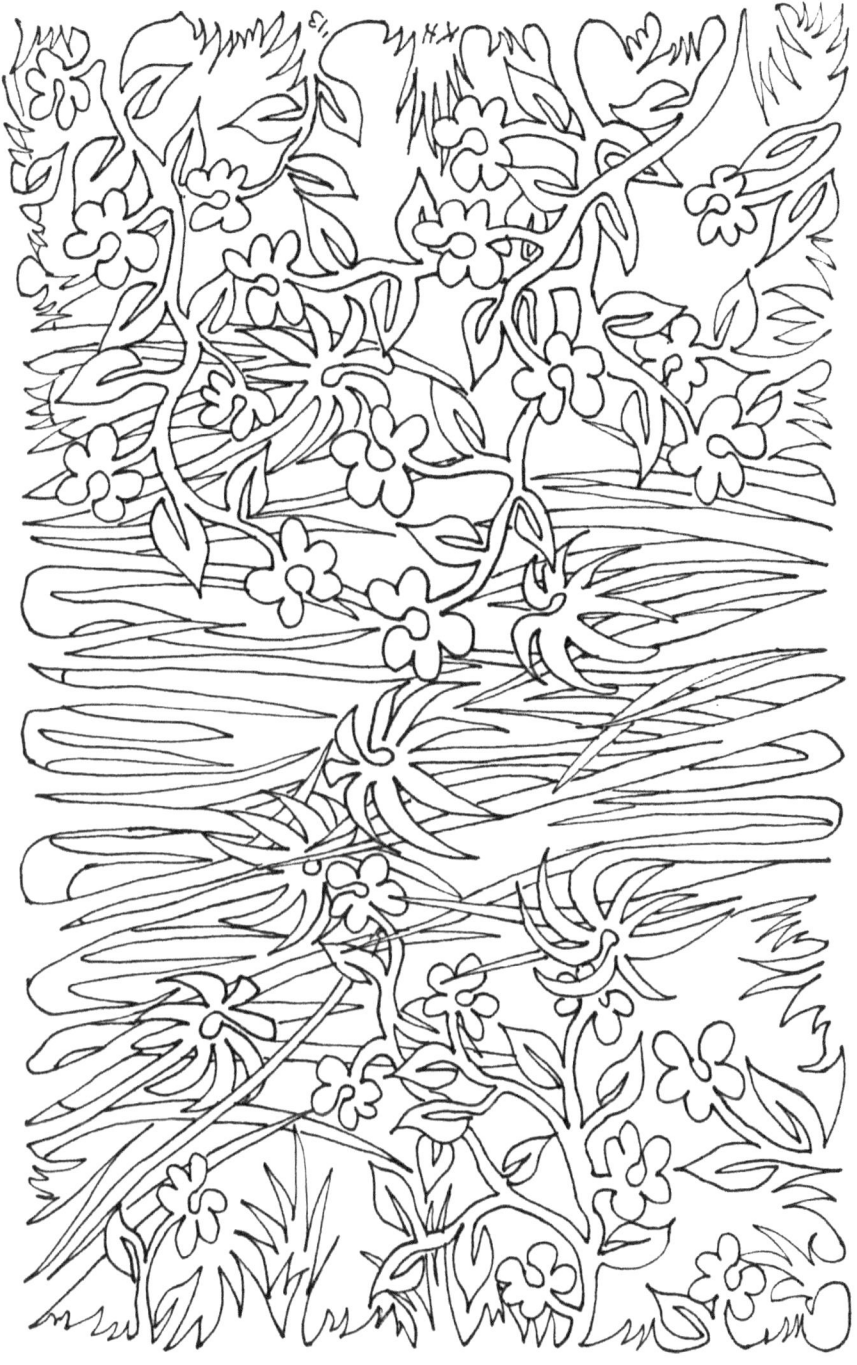

Kathy Carman Henderson

Flow & Flowers

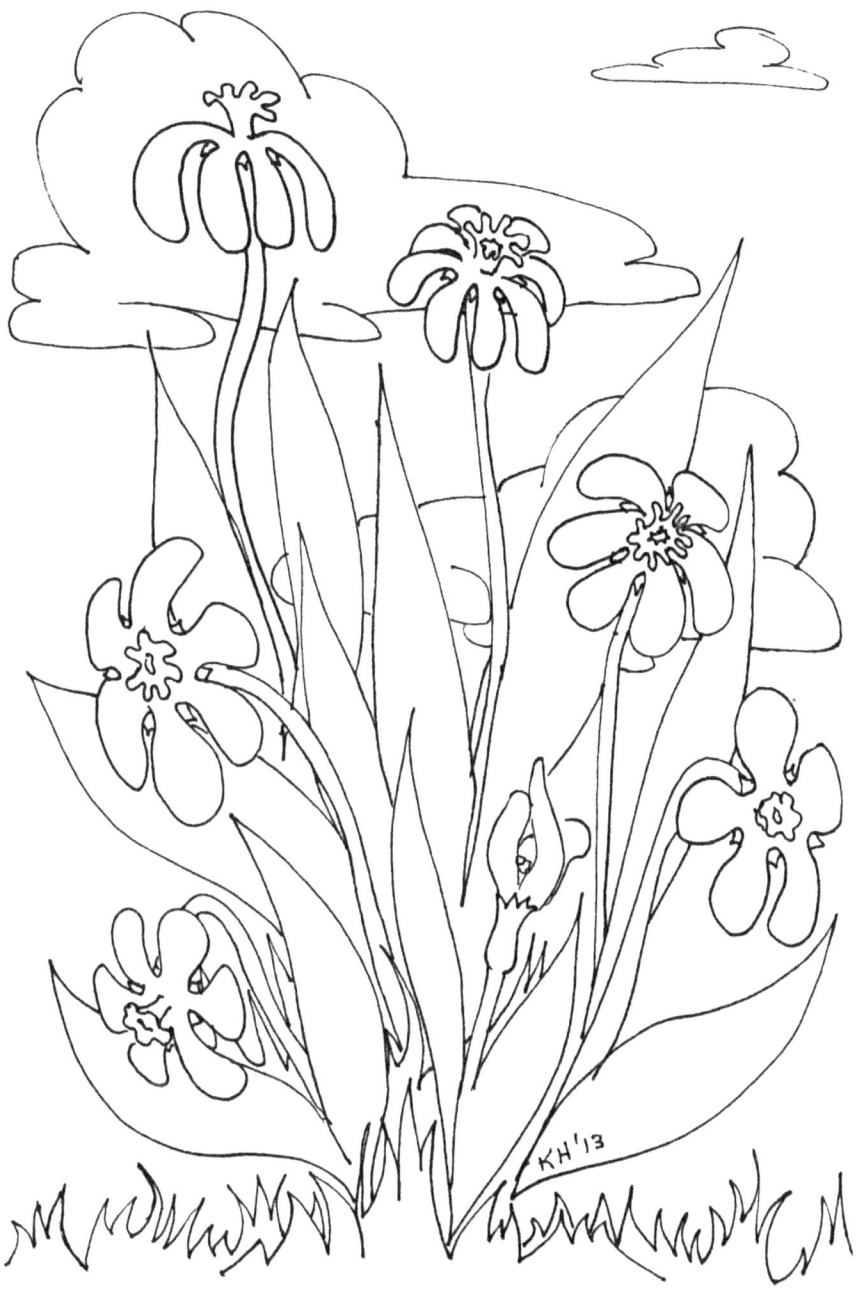

Kathy Carman Henderson

Flow & Flowers

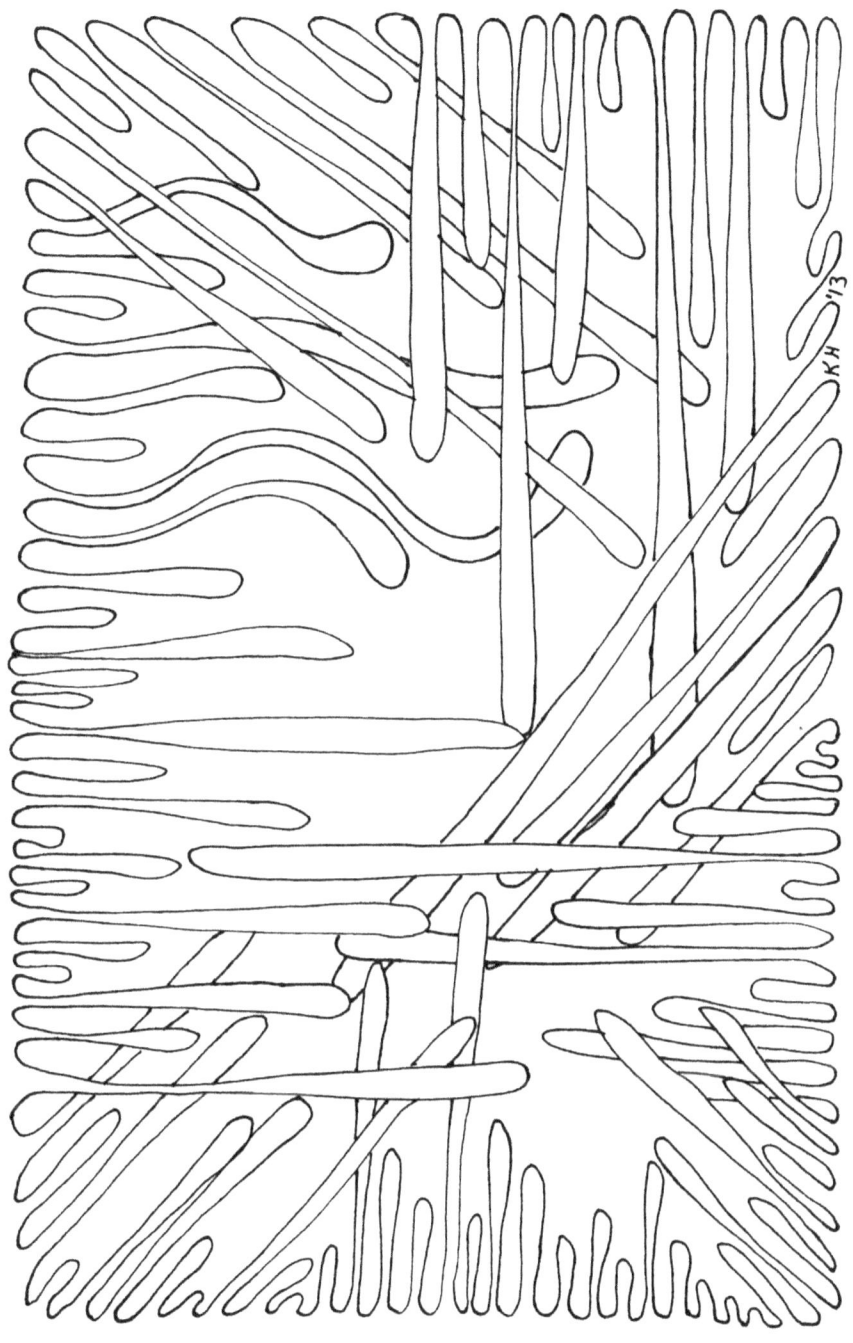

Kathy Carman Henderson

Flow & Flowers

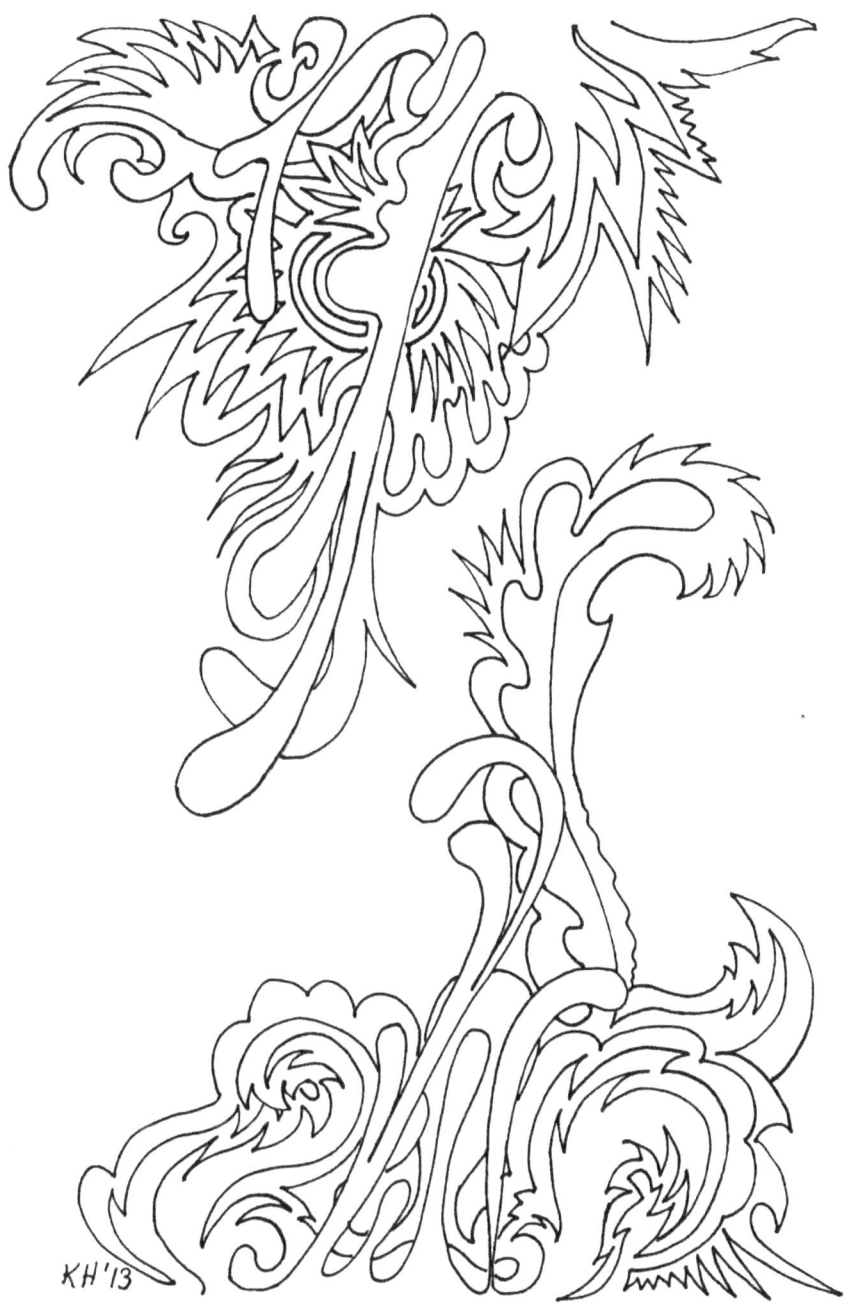

Kathy Carman Henderson

Flow & Flowers

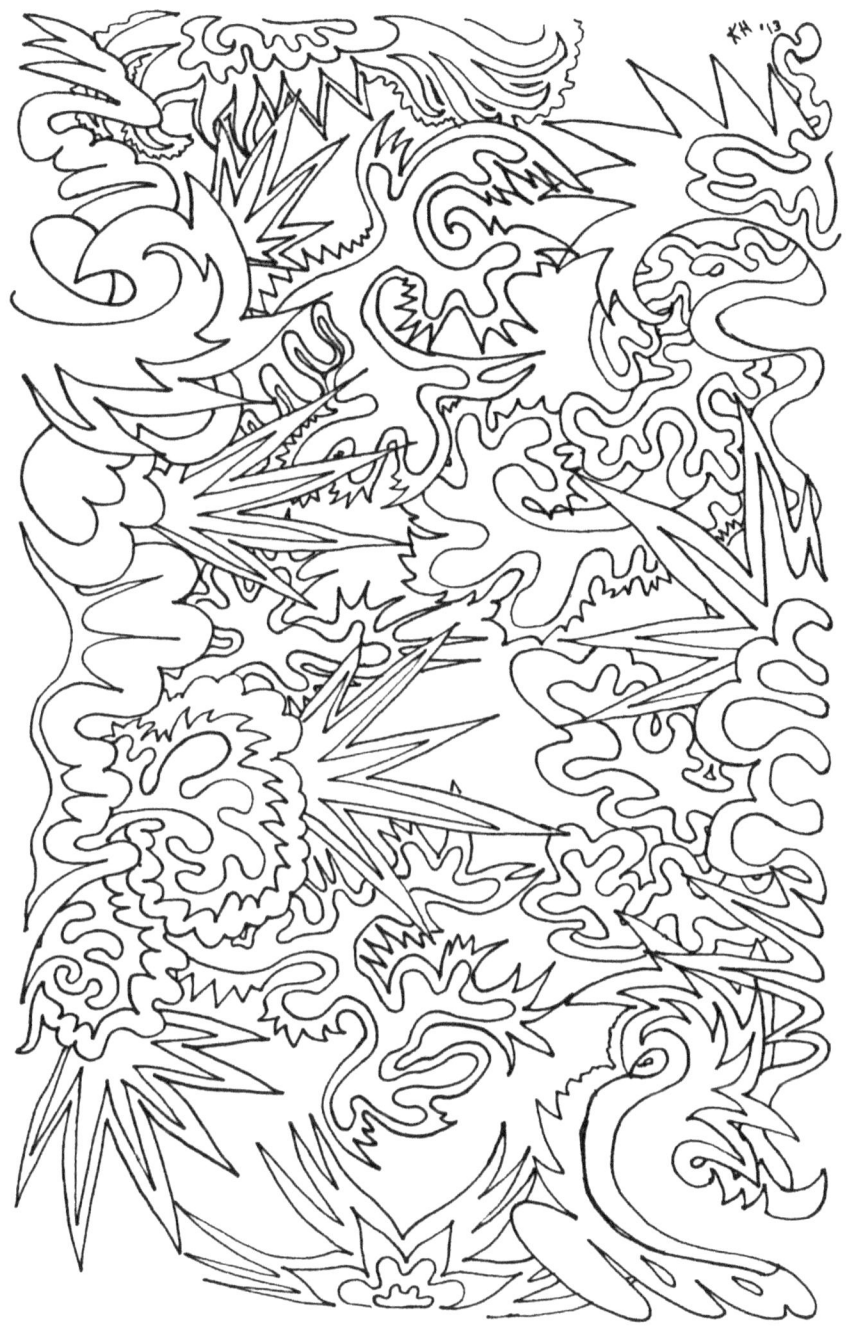

Kathy Carman Henderson

Flow & Flowers

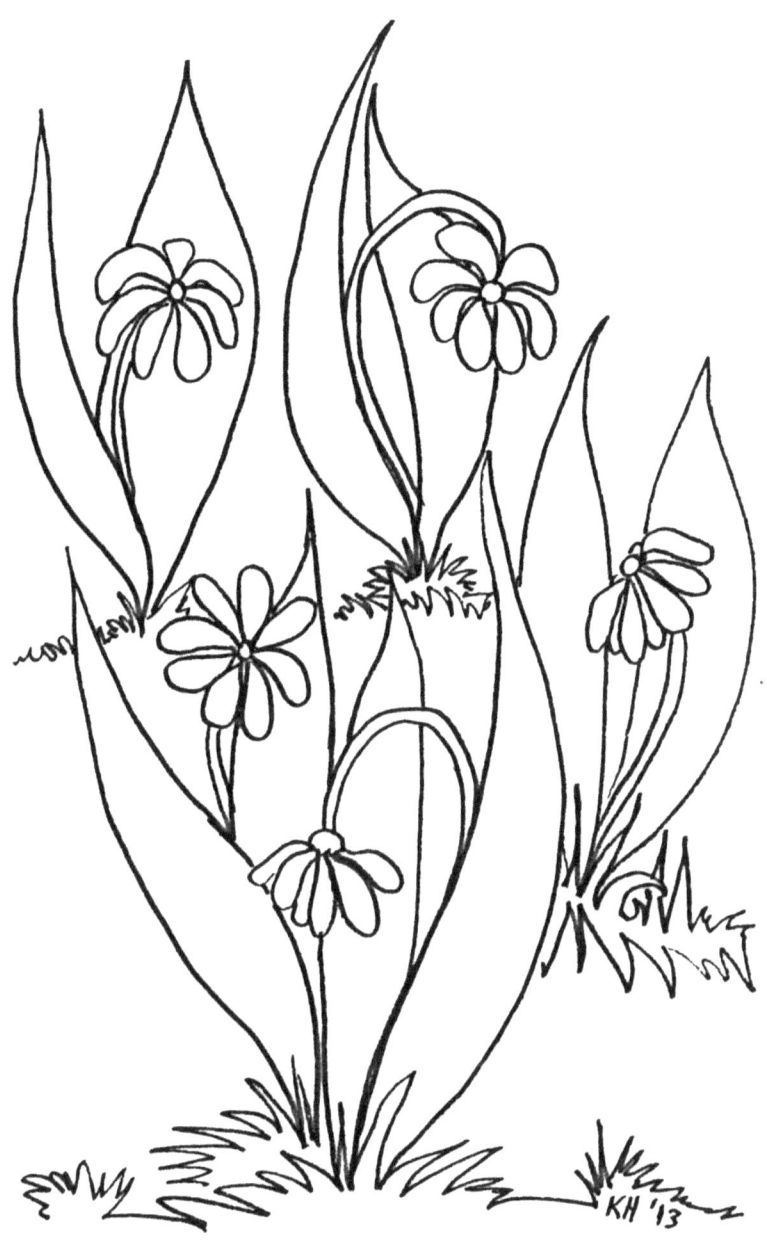

Kathy Carman Henderson

Flow & Flowers

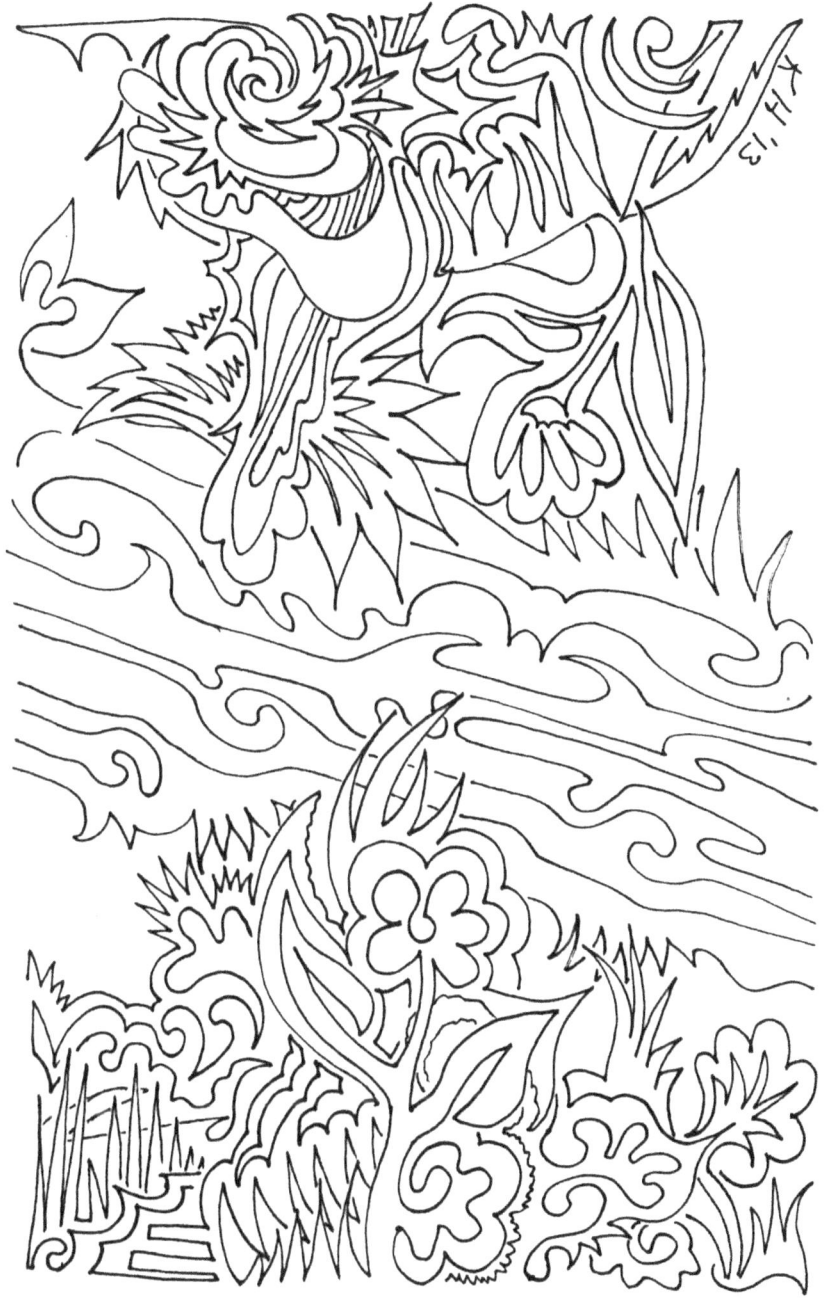

Kathy Carman Henderson

Flow & Flowers

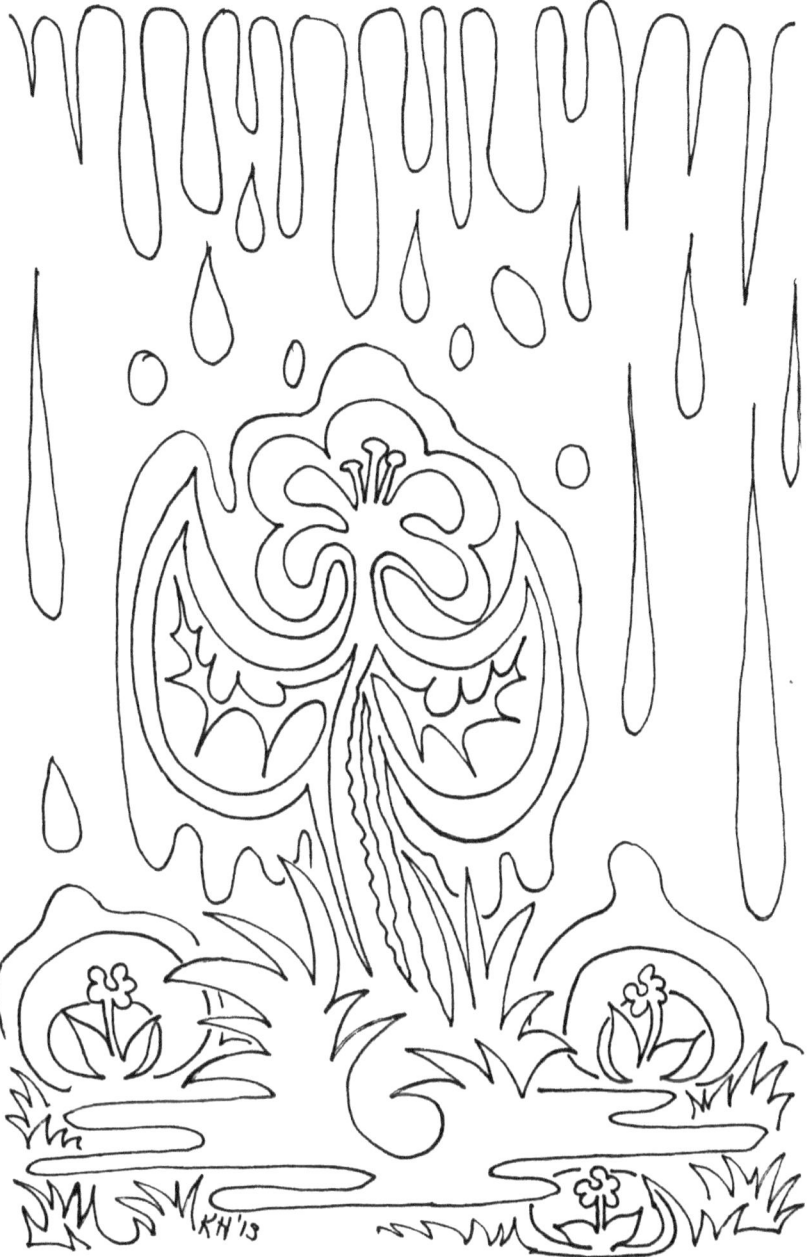

Kathy Carman Henderson

Flow & Flowers

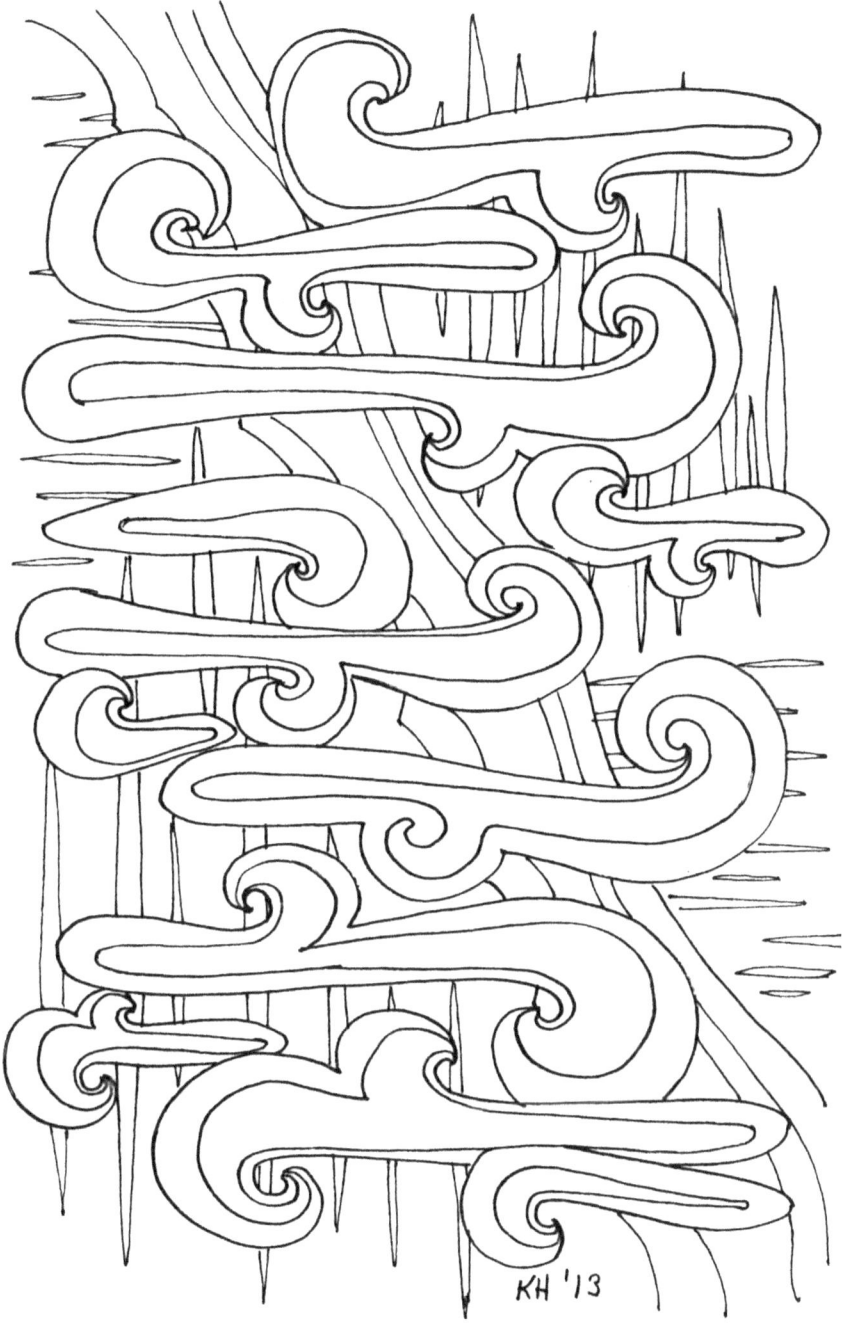

Kathy Carman Henderson

Flow & Flowers

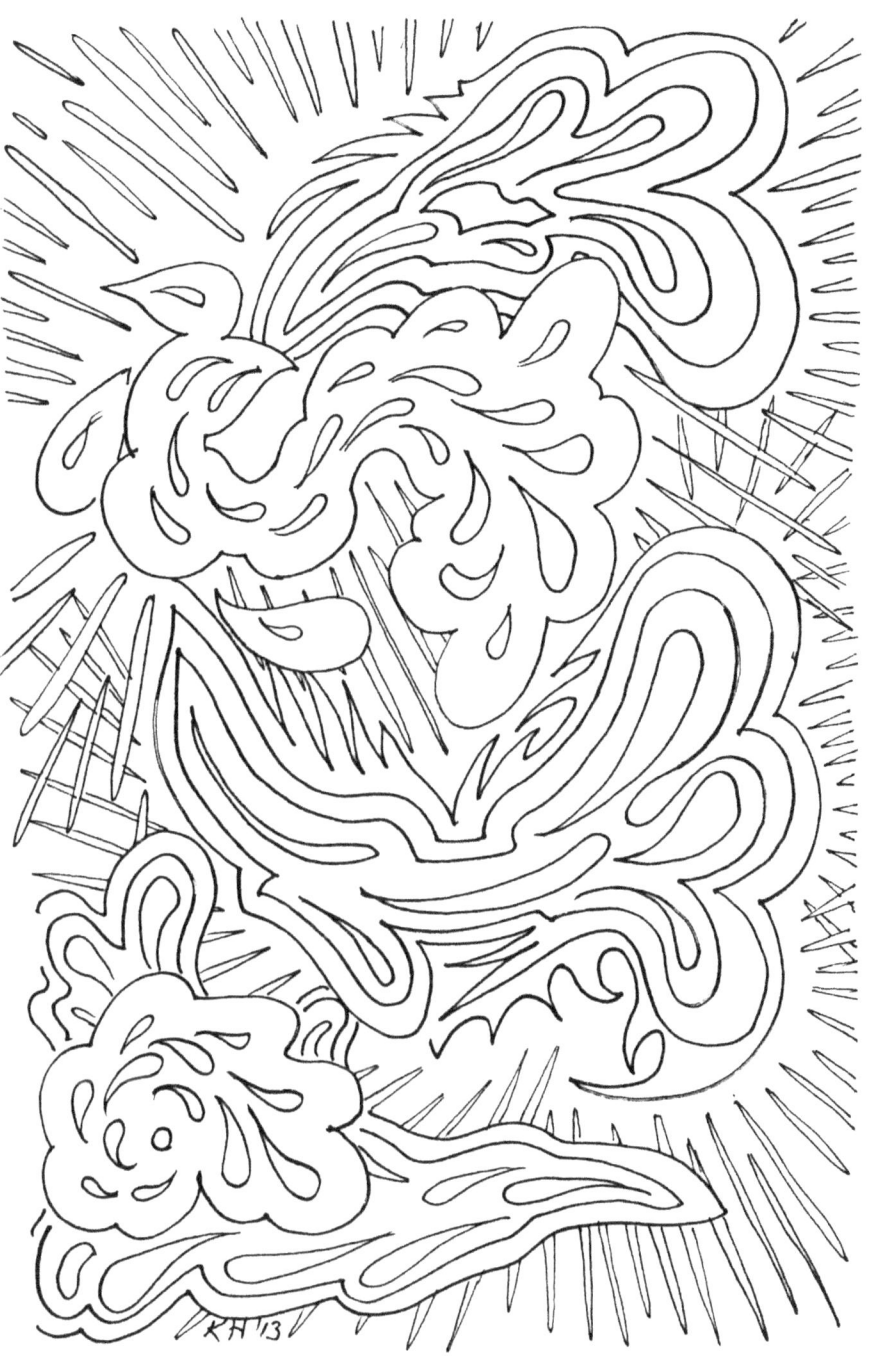

Kathy Carman Henderson

Flow & Flowers

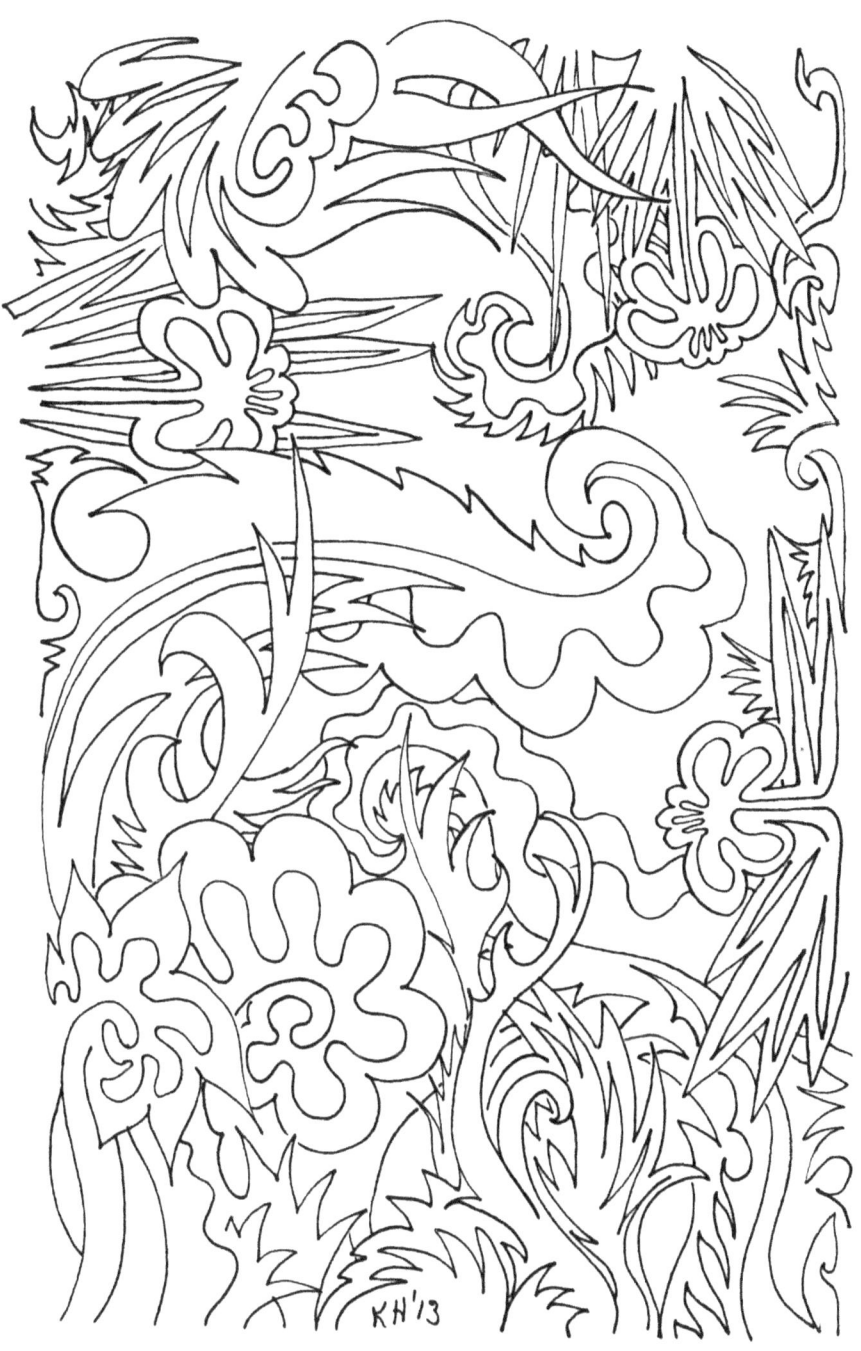

Kathy Carman Henderson

Flow & Flowers

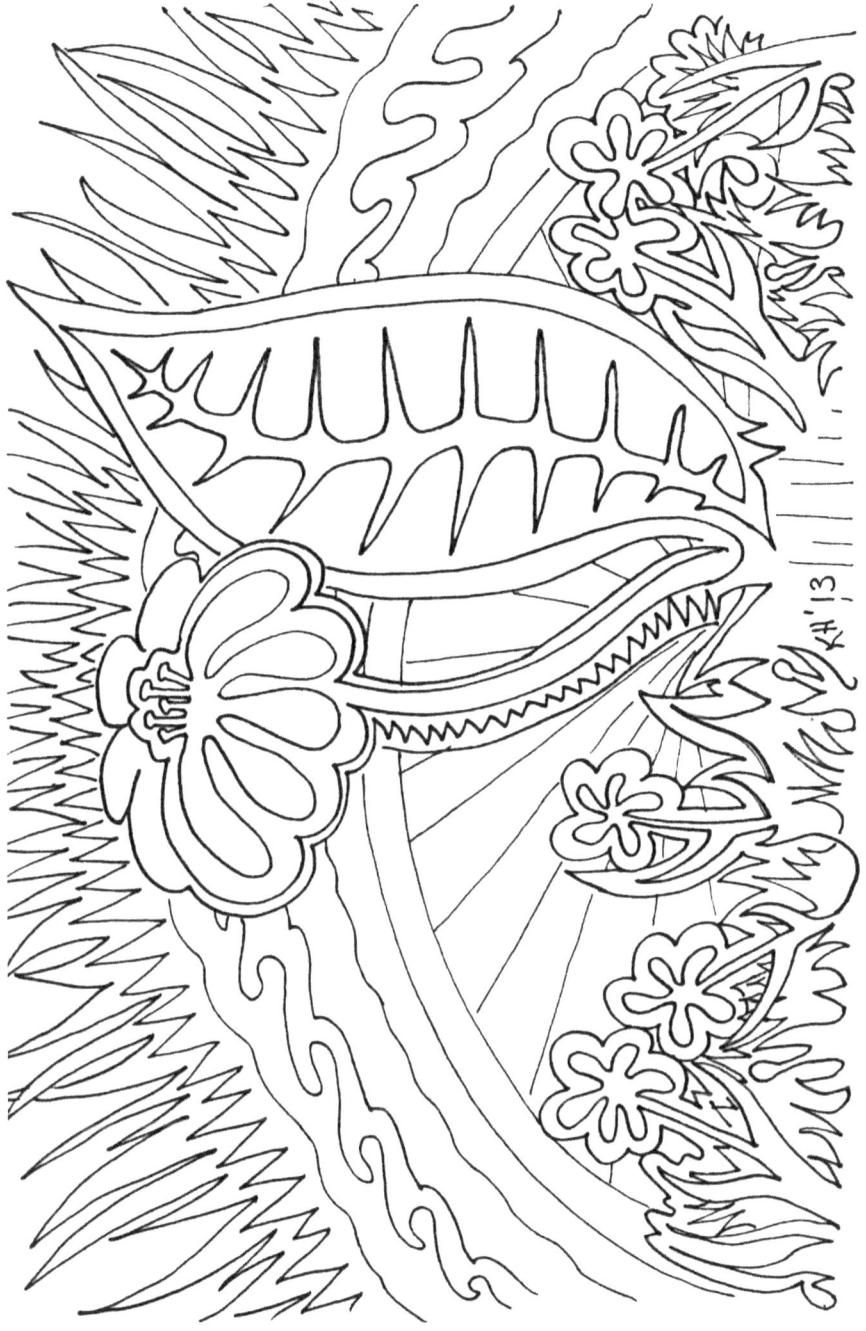

Kathy Carman Henderson

Flow & Flowers

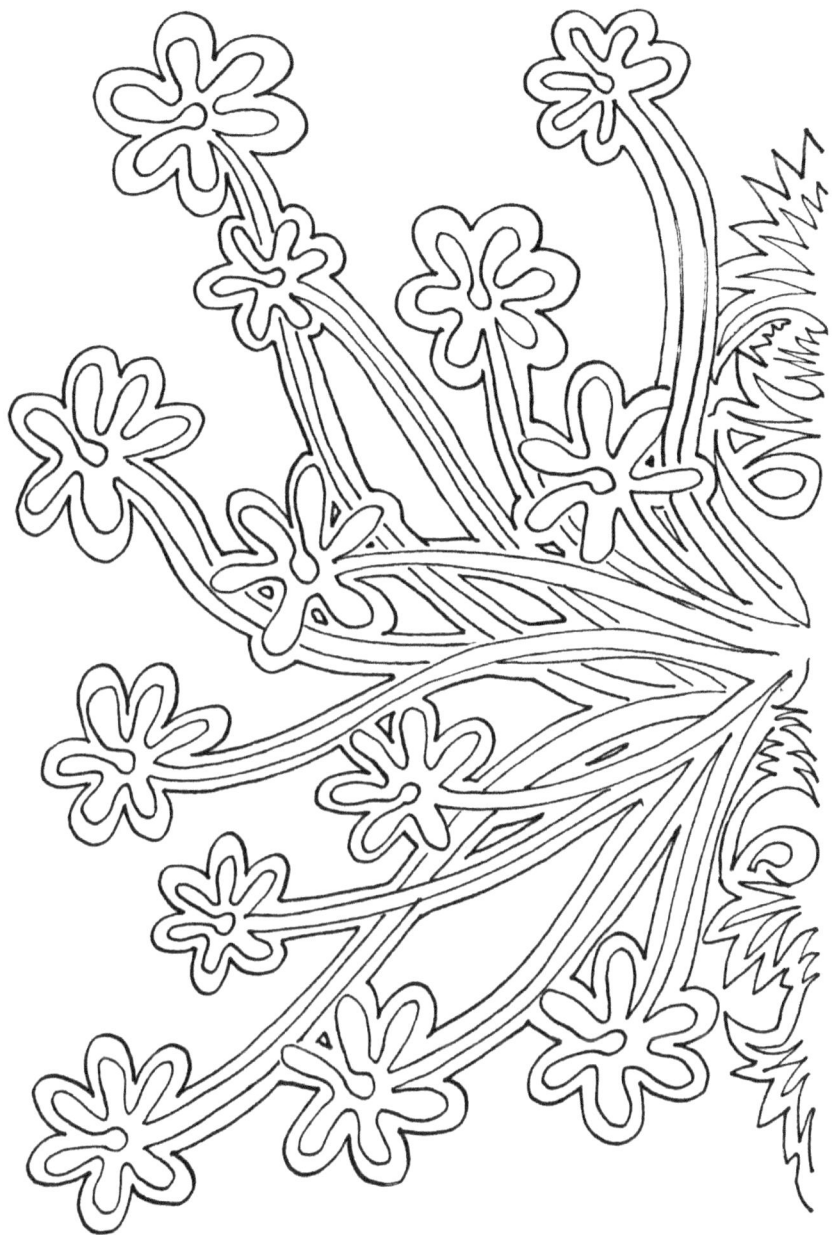

Kathy Carman Henderson

Flow & Flowers

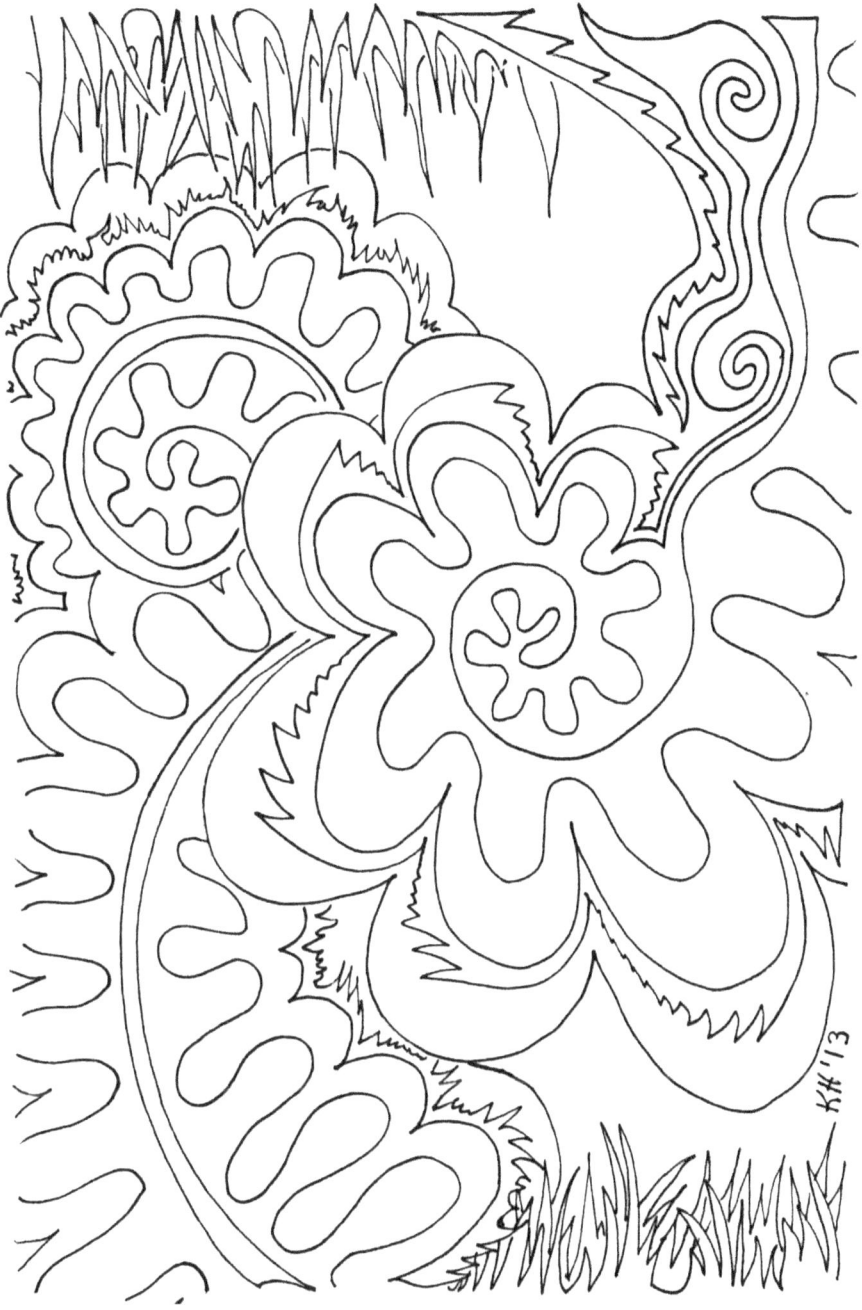

Kathy Carman Henderson

Flow & Flowers

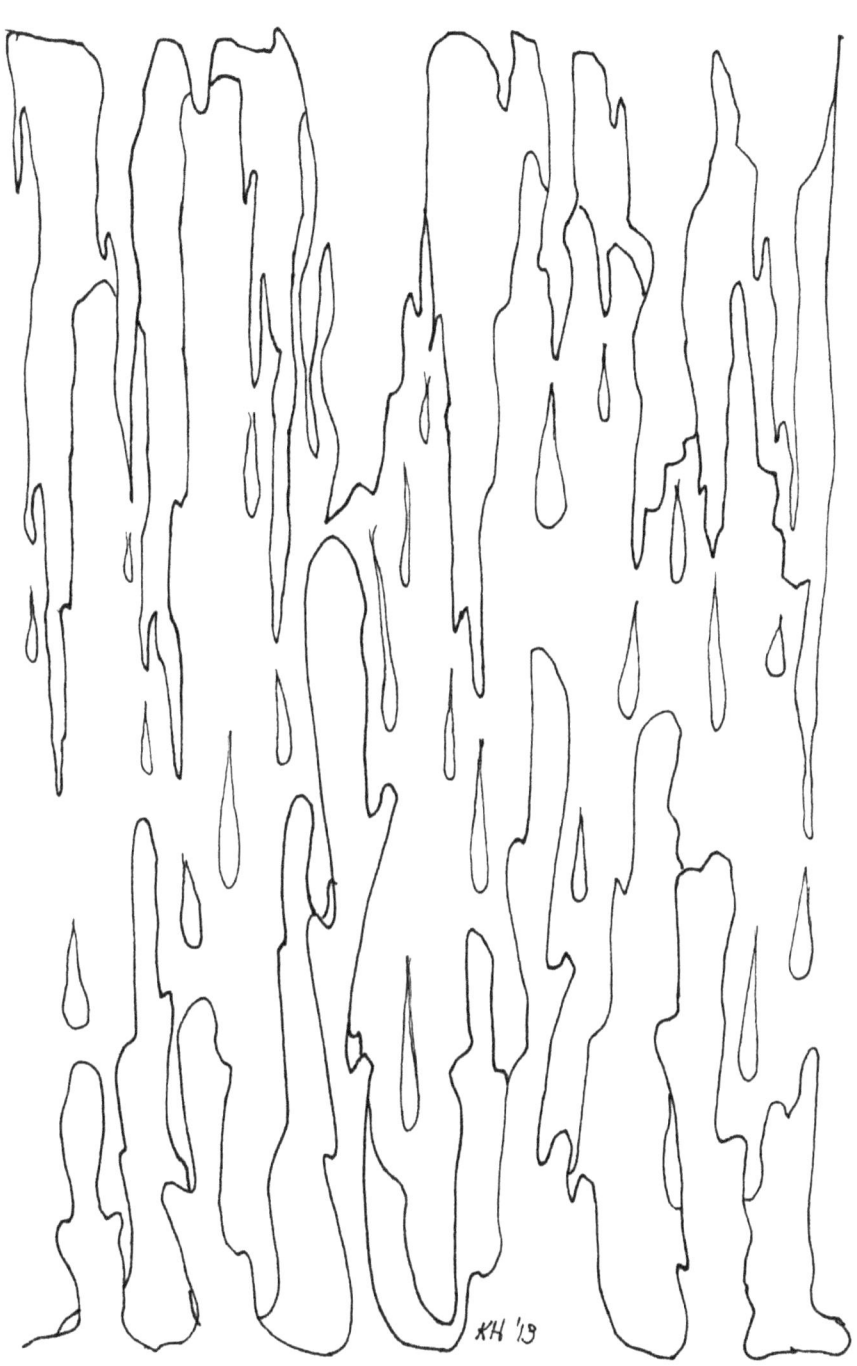

Kathy Carman Henderson

Flow & Flowers

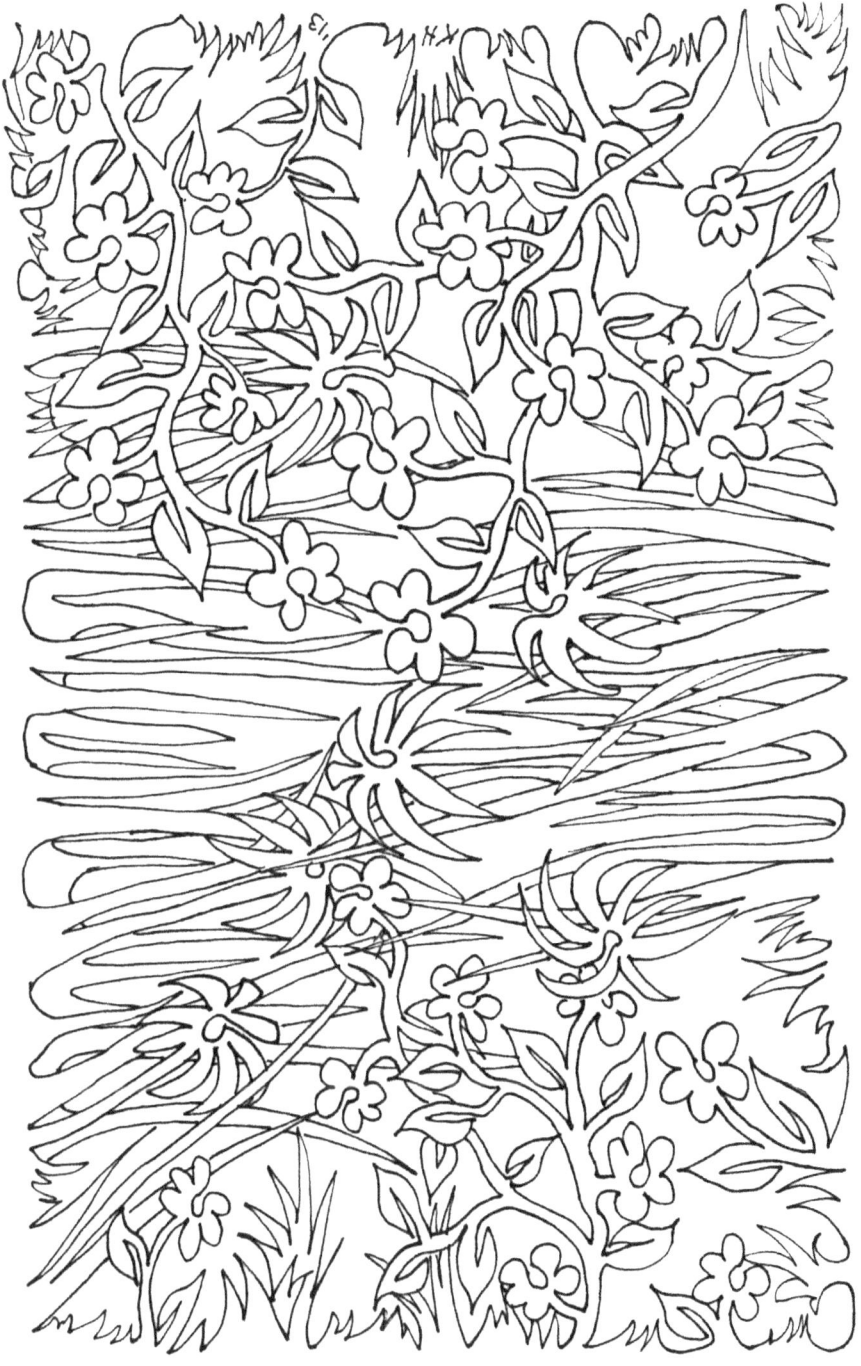

Kathy Carman Henderson

Flow & Flowers

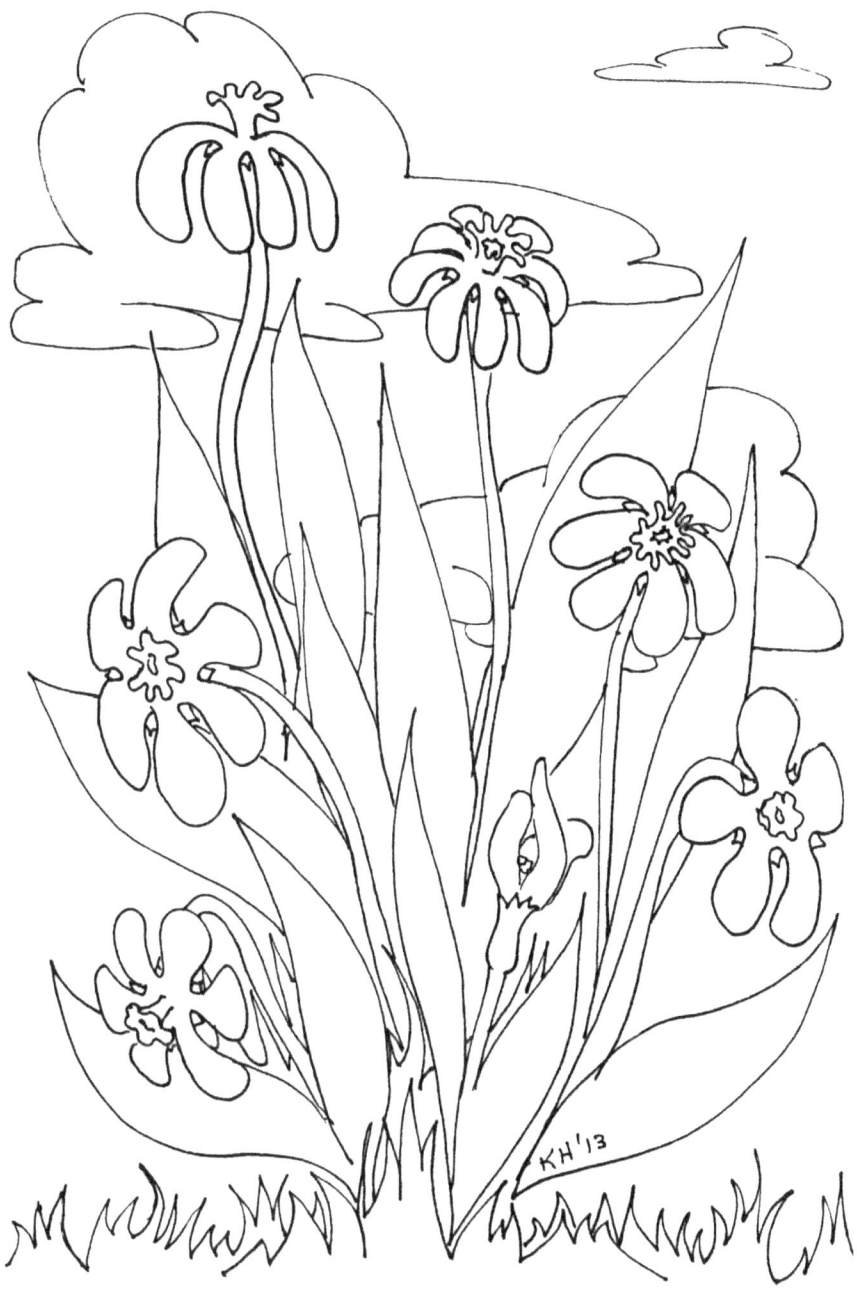

Kathy Carman Henderson

Flow & Flowers

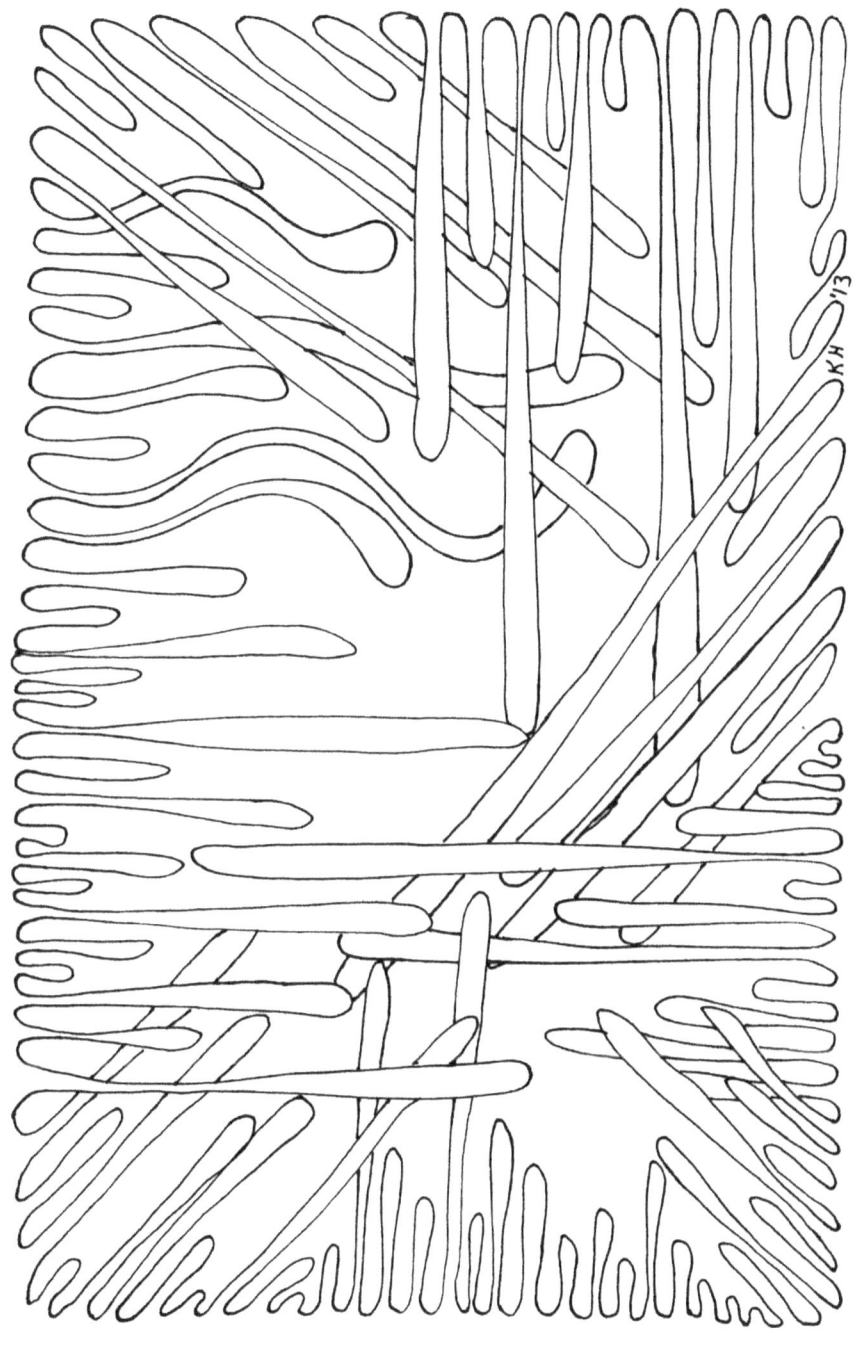

Kathy Carman Henderson

Flow & Flowers

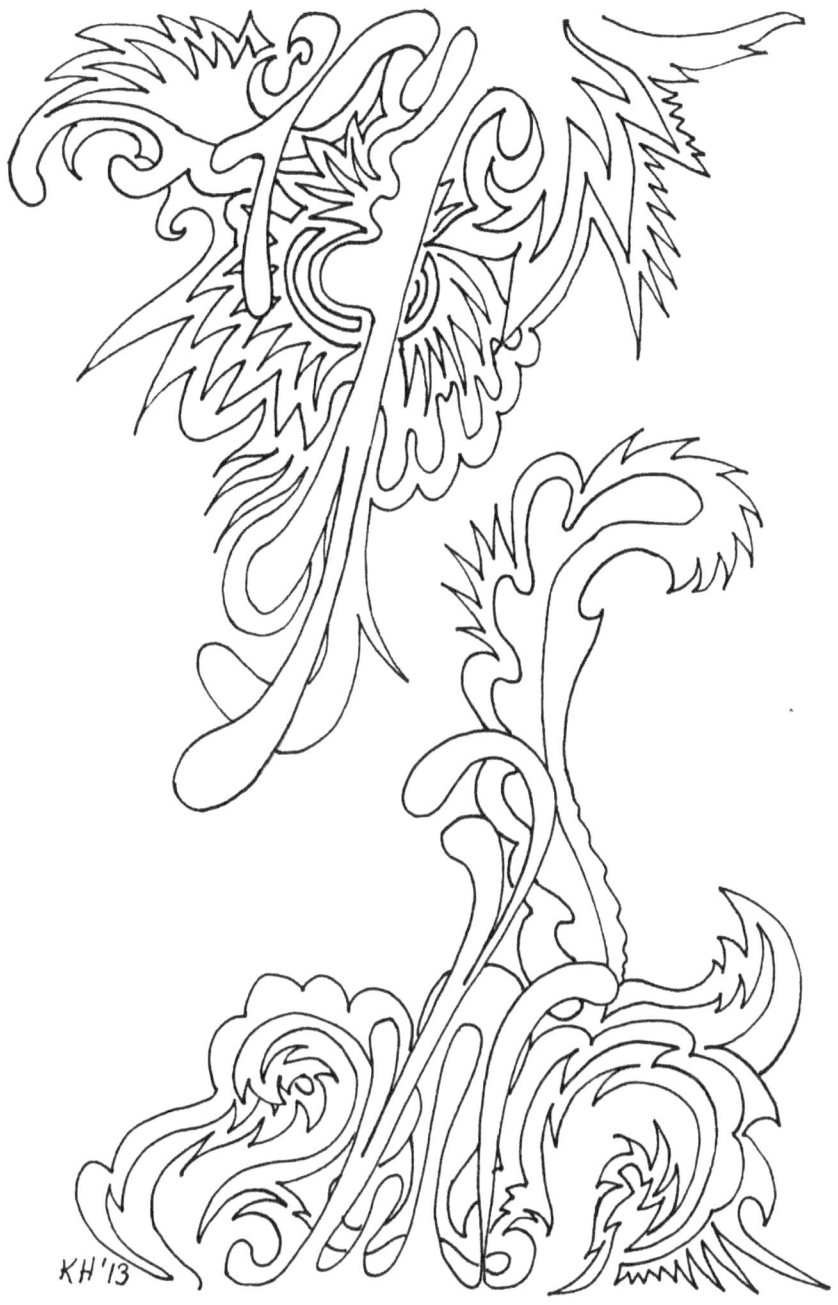

Kathy Carman Henderson

Flow & Flowers

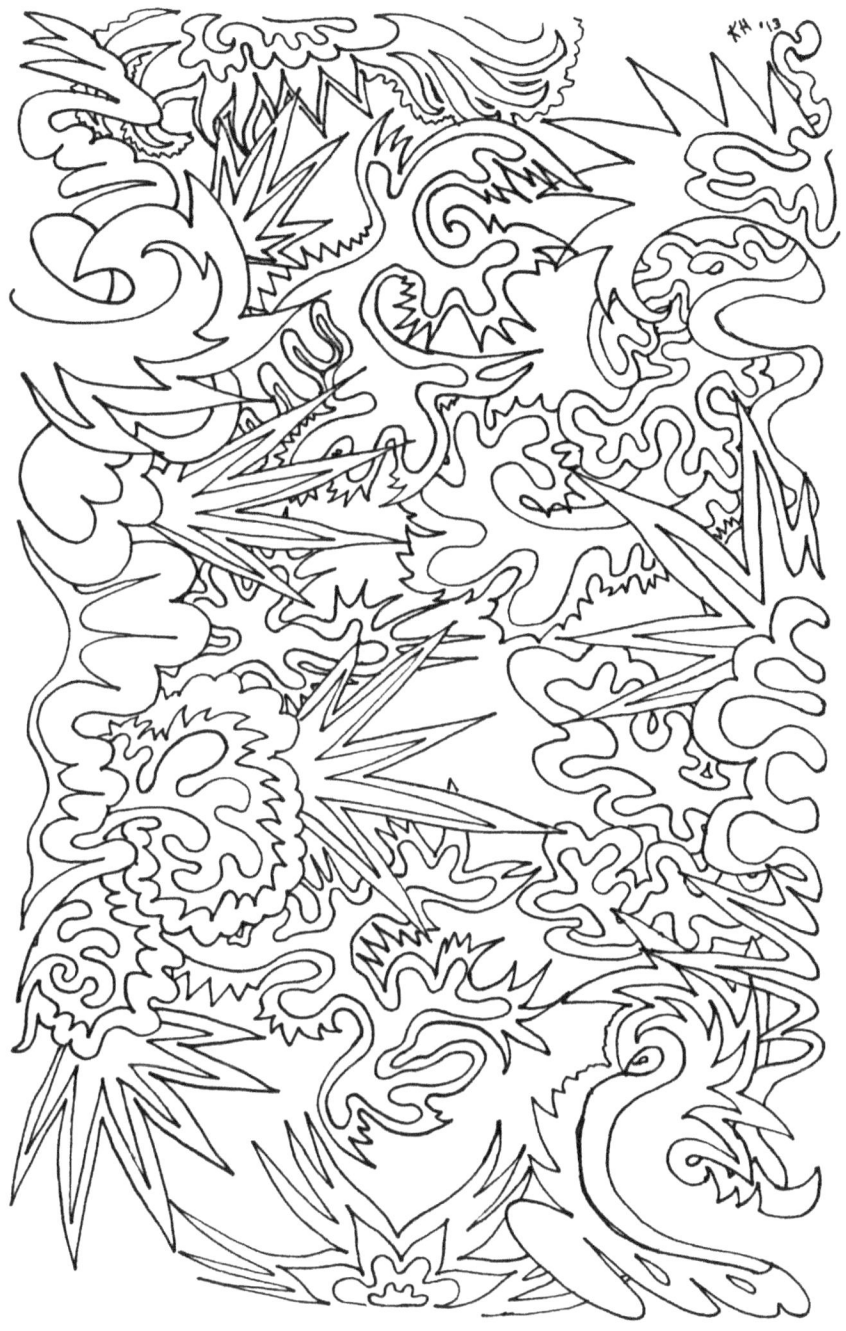

Kathy Carman Henderson

Flow & Flowers

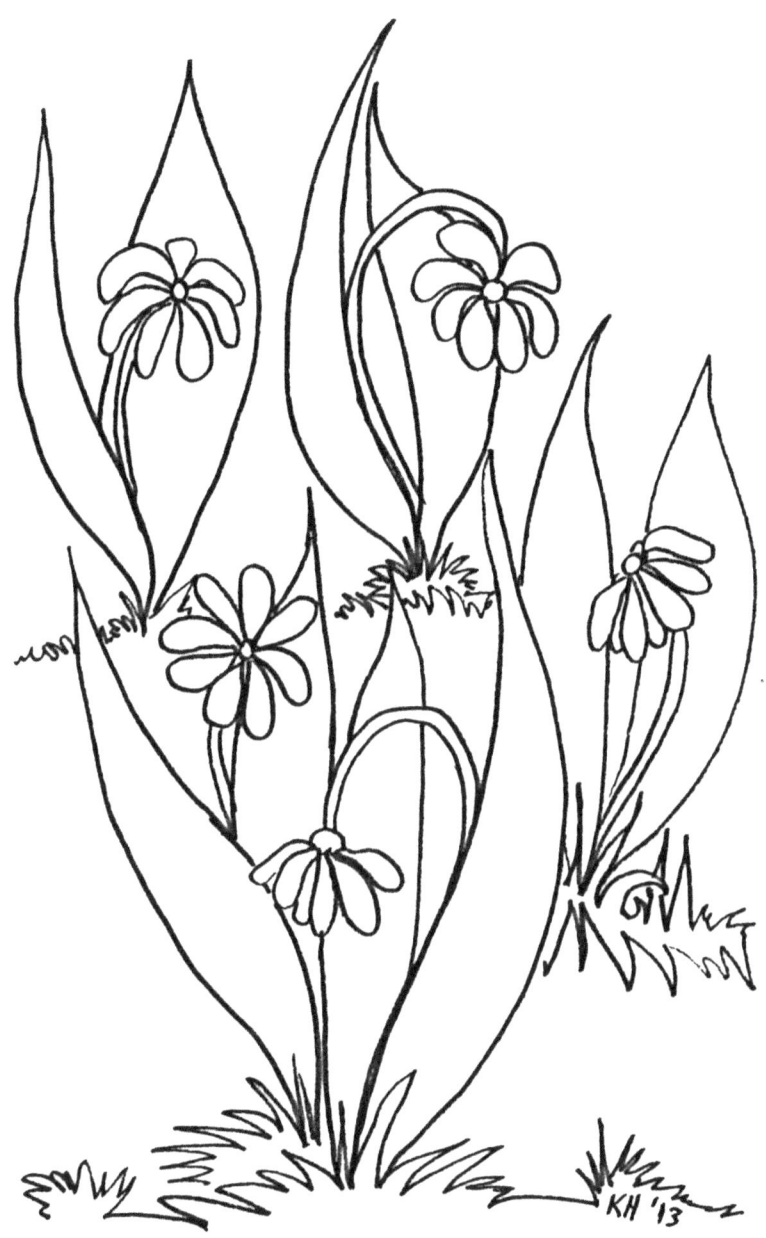

Kathy Carman Henderson

Flow & Flowers

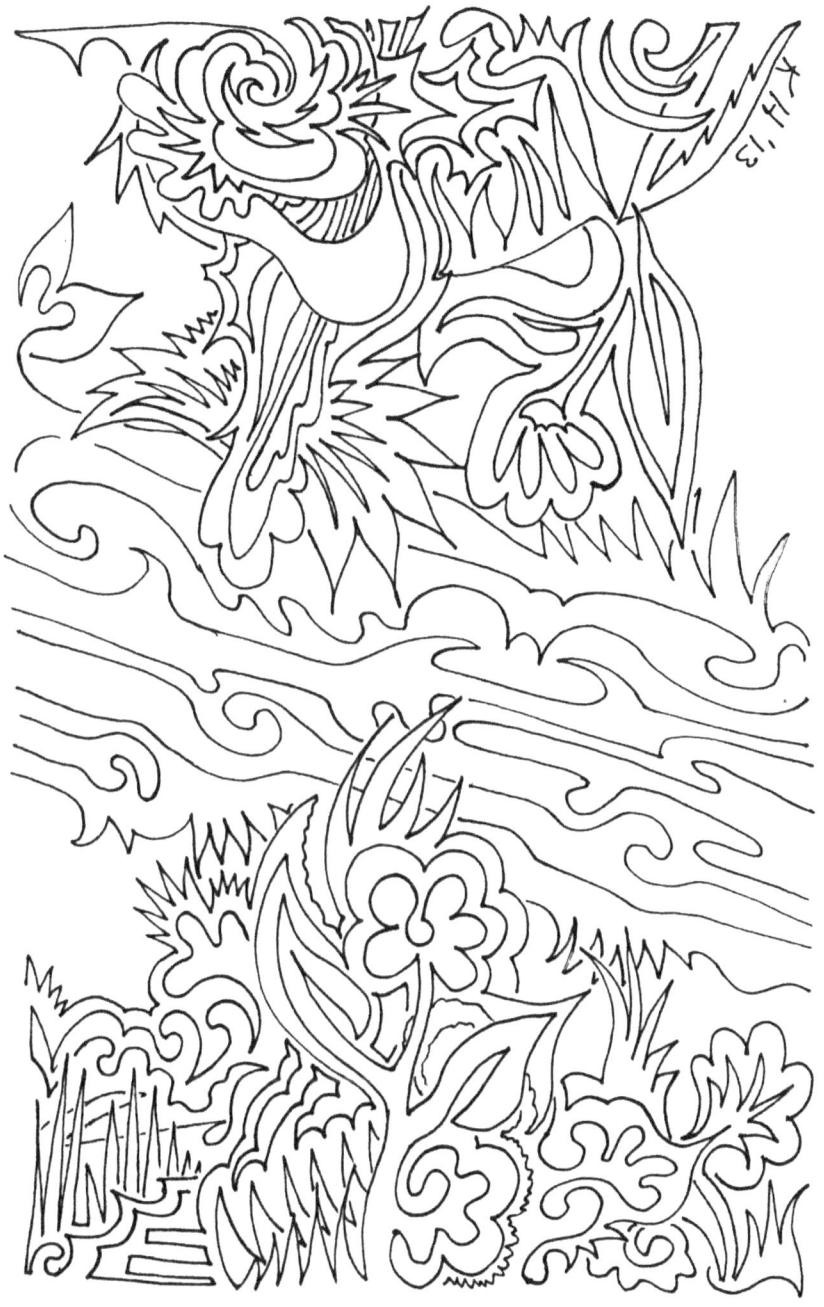

Kathy Carman Henderson

Flow & Flowers

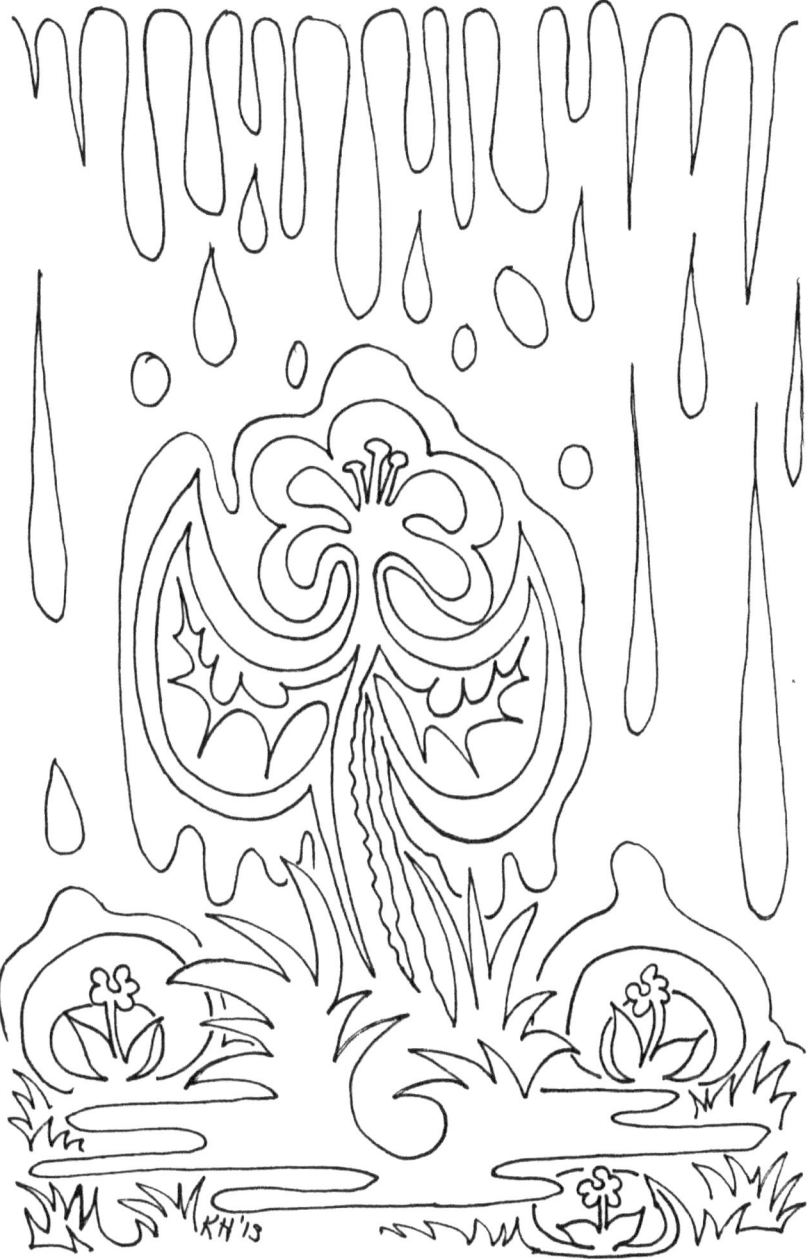

Kathy Carman Henderson

Flow & Flowers

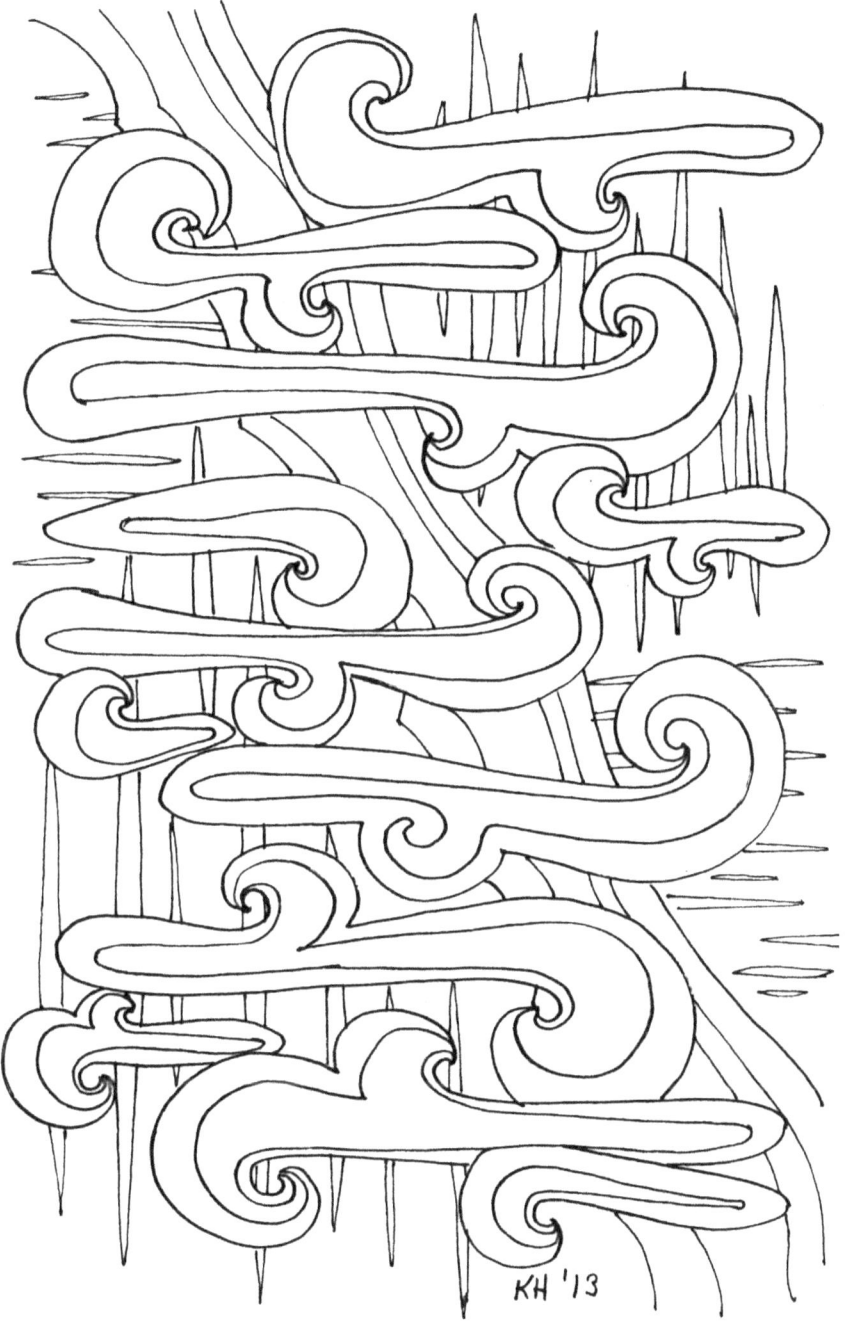

Kathy Carman Henderson

Flow & Flowers

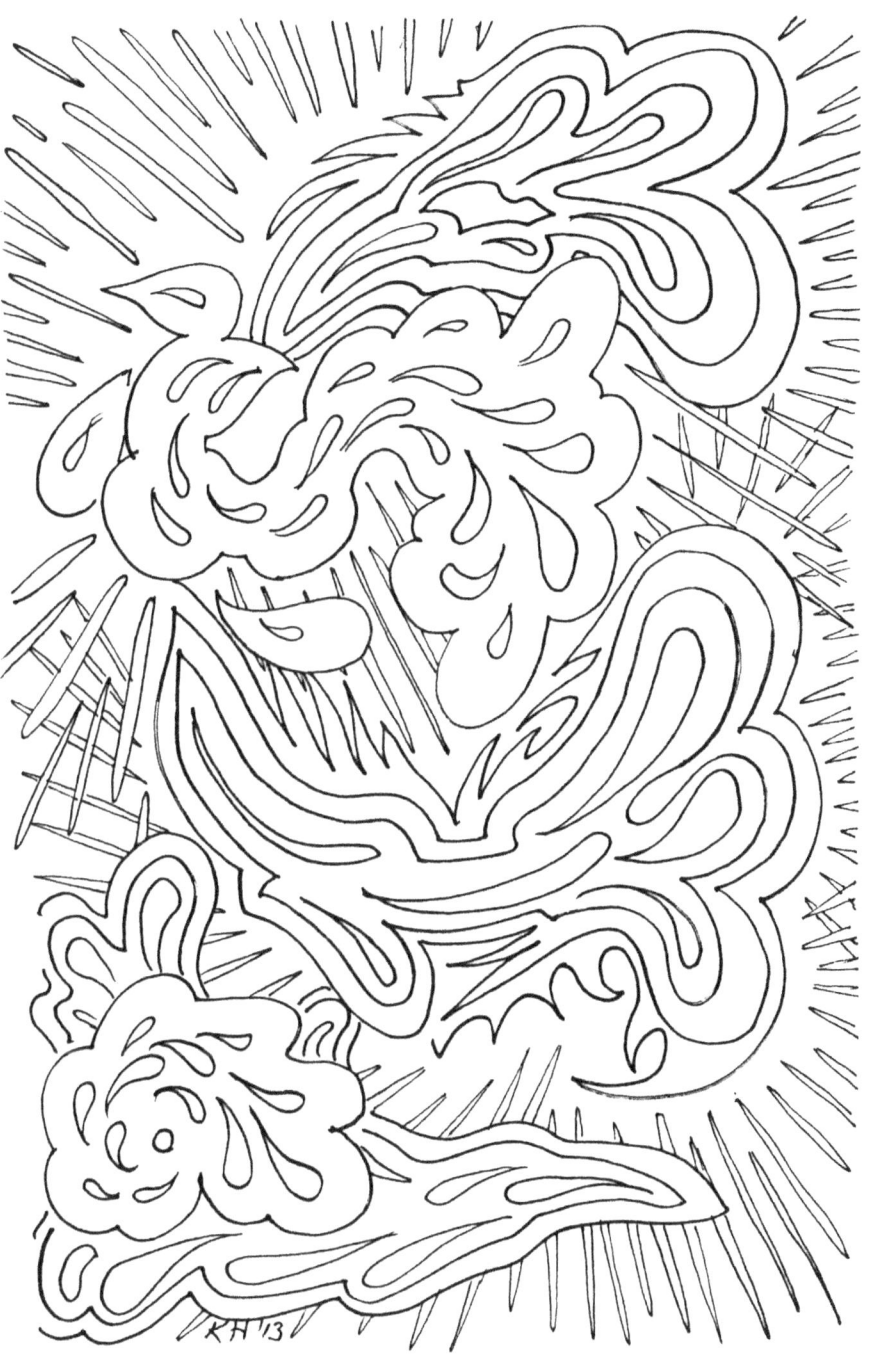

Kathy Carman Henderson is an author, illustrator, and teacher. She started drawing as a young child and continues to find it a valuable part of her life.

Other titles from her include:

Art Coloring Books:
Flowers & Flair

Stories to Learn and Draw by:
The Walking Vegetables
The One You Don't See Coming
The Tiger's Whisker

Fiction Travel Adventure:
Costa Rican Adventure with Ben and Gretchen

Inspirational:
Party of the Ages

For Future Problem Solving International:
Treffinger, Don. **Tools for Problem Solvers,** (Kathy was a contributing author)

Books illustrated for author Edna Creekmore Carman:
A Day of Rest
Tender Twig

www.ingramcontent.com/pod-product-compliance
Lightning Source LLC
Chambersburg PA
CBHW071811170526
45167CB00003B/1261